MUSLIM IMMIGRANTS
IN THEIR SHOES

BY AMY C. REA

Published by The Child's World®
1980 Lookout Drive • Mankato, MN 56003-1705
800-599-READ • www.childsworld.com

Content Consultant: Turan Kayaoglu, Professor & Associate Vice Chancellor for
Research, University of Washington

Photographs ©: Shutterstock Images, cover, 1, 22, 24; Istanbul Photos/Shutterstock
Images, 6, 8; Kevin Wolf/AP Images, 9; Jim Watson/AFP/Getty Images, 11; Ford Motor
Company/AP Images, 12; Rawpixel.com/Shutterstock Images, 14; M. Spencer Green/
AP Images, 15; Anthony Lanzilote/Getty Images News/Getty Images, 16; Suman
Bhaumik/Shutterstock Images, 18; PeopleImages/iStockphoto, 20; Red Line Editorial,
21; Jim Mone/AP Images, 26; Rick Bowmer/AP Images, 28

ISBN 9781503828001
LCCN 2018944222

Printed in the United States of America
PA02394

ABOUT THE AUTHOR

Amy C. Rea grew up in northern Minnesota and now lives in a Minneapolis
suburb with her husband, two sons, and dog. She writes frequently about
traveling around Minnesota.

TABLE OF CONTENTS

FAST FACTS

Islam in the United States

- Islam is the religion that **Muslim** people practice.

- The first large group of Muslims came to the United States in the 1600s. They were from Africa and were forced into slavery.

- In 1930, the Nation of Islam was founded in the United States. It was an African-American religious movement that used many Islamic elements.

- Ramadan is the Islamic holy month. During Ramadan, Muslims don't drink or eat between sunrise and sunset. This allows Muslims to focus on their faith.

History of Muslim Immigration

- Until 1965, the few Muslim immigrants who came to the United States were from the Soviet Union after World War II (1939–1945). They were trying to escape religious injustice and Russian takeover of Muslim regions.

- The U.S. Hart-Celler Act passed in 1965. It opened the doors for Muslims from many countries to come to the United States.

TIMELINE

1878–1924: Muslim immigrants from the Middle East begin arriving in the United States. Most settle in Ohio, Michigan, Iowa, and the Dakotas.

1924: Non-European immigration to the United States is restricted by the National Origins Act.

1930s–1940s: Muslim immigrants begin to build **mosques** in the United States.

1965–2000: After the 1965 Hart-Celler Act becomes law, more than 1.1 million new Muslims arrive in the United States.

2007: The first Muslim American is elected to Congress: Keith Ellison. Ellison uses Thomas Jefferson's copy of the **Quran** to swear his oath of office.

2018: The U.S. Supreme Court supports President Donald Trump's travel ban. The ban restricts travel from several Muslim countries, including Iran, Syria, and Somalia.

Chapter 1

THE FIRST MUSLIM IMMIGRANTS ARRIVE

In the late 1800s, the Muslim man sat down at his friend's home in New York City and looked at the faces that surrounded him. He folded his hands and set them on his lap. He listened intently as some of the men spoke about their lives in the United States. He was tired after his long day of work, but he soaked up every word the men said.

In the late 1800s, immigrants came to the United States from the Ottoman Empire, which covered many countries including what is now Syria and Libya. They did not feel safe in their **homeland** anymore. They came to the United States and earned money however they could. Many Muslim immigrants at this time did back-breaking work as miners. They also got jobs in factories and grocery stores or worked as traveling **peddlers**.

The Muslim man was growing tired of that hard life. Sometimes people called him names. He knew they called other immigrants names, too, especially the Irish. But the hours he spent every day trying to earn enough money to eat was exhausting. Some people he knew gave up and returned to the Ottoman Empire.

But now someone in his group was talking about moving to Iowa. They could start farms or establish stores there. And maybe people would be more accepting in that state. In 1885, the Muslim man was with a group of people who set out for Iowa. They arrived in Cedar Rapids and decided to settle there.

The Muslim man decided to try farming. It was hard work, but he loved the feeling of having dirt under his hands and knowing that he owned the land.

The summer farming season could get hot. Sweat beaded on his forehead as he worked. But he thought the heat was no worse than what he'd grown up with across the ocean. He began to enjoy his new life.

▲ **The majority of people who lived in the Ottoman Empire were Muslims.**

▲ **Muslims in Cedar Rapids gather and celebrate their religion.**

He also enjoyed the small Muslim community in Cedar Rapids. The people who came to Iowa with him worked together. They also worshipped together, but they wished the town they lived in had a mosque. Other religions in Cedar Rapids had churches where the people could gather. To build a mosque would take money and time.

The Muslim man married a Muslim woman in the community and they had children. He hoped someday to have a place to take his family to worship.

It was not until 1925 that his community was able to rent a building to serve as a temporary mosque. Having even a temporary mosque was encouraging. Together, the group began developing plans for building a permanent mosque.

Through the years, the Muslims and Christians in Cedar Rapids supported each other. As plans for the mosque came along, another religious group planned its own new building. When the St. George's Orthodox Church was completed, the Muslims purchased a cross to give to the church. When the mosque opened in 1934, St. George's helped the Muslims celebrate. Later, members from both religions served in the U.S. military during World War II.

As the Muslim man grew old, he thought about the people who had come to the United States but then left. He was glad he had not left. The Muslim man had achieved much in Cedar Rapids.

"[My husband] always said, 'Don't be like an ostrich, and just bury your head in the sand. Go out and speak to others. Be involved in your community. That's the only way they are going to know who we are.'"[1]

—Aziza (Betty) Igram, a Muslim immigrant who arrived in Cedar Rapids in the 1940s

▲ **The Mother Mosque of America in Cedar Rapids is the oldest standing mosque in the United States.**

Coming to the city had helped him find the kind of life he had hoped for. He was proud to be an American Muslim.

Throughout the 2000s, the mosque in Cedar Rapids, the Mother Mosque of America, continued to bring joy to the community. One Muslim leader of the mosque, Taha Tawil, said the building represents "freedom, respect, integrity, and hard work."[2]

Chapter 2

LOOKING FOR A BETTER LIFE

The Henry Ford plant outside of Detroit, Michigan, was a large building and very noisy. Inside, men raced to keep Model T cars moving down the line. Each man had his own task to do over and over again. One man would fit pieces together. The next man would bolt those pieces into place. A third man would screw nuts over the bolts.

◄ The Ford assembly line decreased the amount of time it took to make cars.

As the cars came together, there were clanging noises from metal parts being fitted. There were shouts from workers talking to each other. Sometimes supervisors would talk to employees or tell them to work faster.

In 1913, Ford had launched an assembly line. Before the assembly line came along, each car was put together by skilled workers who had special training. But now people without that training could easily assemble cars. Each person had just one task that he did over and over. Many jobs were filled by immigrants who had left behind countries where they could not find work.

> "[My father] prayed alone on his rug every Friday at sunset. Then he would give **alms** in the form of fruit and candy to the neighbor's children."[3]
>
> —*Lurey Khan, the daughter of a Muslim man who came to the United States in 1929*

The work was hard and often dull, but one young Muslim man was thrilled to get a job at the plant. He had left his home in Syria, desperate to find steady work to earn a living.

▲ **Many Muslim kids learn how to recite the Quran at an early age.**

There weren't many jobs in Syria. He was not the only Muslim to arrive in the Detroit area looking for work. Some people came from parts of Western and Eastern Europe. Others, such as the young Muslim man, came from the Middle East.

The man was thrilled to have a good-paying job. But there was something bothering him. He knew many other Muslims who lived in the Detroit area. Some of them had also moved there to find jobs at the Ford plant. The man saw that many of the other Muslims did not practice their religion. They had no gathering place or leader to teach them messages from the Quran.

▲ **The Islamic faith encourages Muslims to pray five times a day.**

There was no one who could perform Islamic marriage or burial ceremonies. Children were being raised without knowing a lot about the religion of their parents and grandparents.

The young Muslim man was troubled. He wanted to be able to practice his faith and have others in the community join him. But he himself did not know how to read. So he decided to learn.

Day after day, he sat down in his rented room after work. He was often exhausted. It would have been easier to just eat a meal and go right to sleep. But he stayed awake, studying his Quran so he could learn to read **Arabic**.

The young Muslim man succeeded and began to offer full Islamic services to his Muslim immigrant neighbors. Those services included handling weddings, funerals, and Islamic education for children. By the 1920s, he was the imam in his community. An imam is a worship leader in the Islamic faith. He provided Islamic services for nearly 50 years, long after he left the Ford plant and began selling food products instead. His job changed. But his determination to provide religious services to his community did not.

◄ **Imams lead prayers at mosques.**

Chapter 3

MUSLIMS FROM ALL OVER THE WORLD

T he day that the young Indian man graduated from college was the best day of his life. His parents smiled throughout the entire ceremony. Their faces shone with pride and his mother had tears of joy in her eyes. The young man felt excited. He had wanted to be an engineer for as long as he could remember.

◀ **More than 100 million Muslims live in India.**

When he was accepted into a college engineering program in India, it was a dream come true.

People all over India wanted to get college degrees. There was only one problem. Colleges and universities were educating more and more people, but there were not enough jobs for all the people who were graduating. The young Indian man's excitement at having an engineering degree began to lessen. Jobs were not easily available. It seemed that every time he applied for a job, there were many other people who also wanted it.

In 1965, the newspaper reported that the U.S. government was changing its laws about immigration. The Hart-Celler Act made it illegal to prohibit immigration by someone based on his or her race, gender, nationality, or place of birth. The young man heard stories of jobs in the United States. There were engineering companies that desperately needed skilled, educated employees. Although it was hard to think about leaving his home, he very much wanted to use his engineering skills.

The young man took a long, difficult journey from India to New York City. After many hours, his plane landed. The day was cold, cloudy, and windy. The young man had been through mild winters in India, but it was bitterly cold in New York.

He was not used to the weather. Still, the promise of a new life was exciting.

Before long, the young man had a job in Chicago, Illinois, as an engineer. The company he worked for had other Muslims working there, too. Some were from India, like him. But there were others from all over the world. He met Muslim immigrants from different parts of Asia, Africa, and Latin America. Many of them had come to the United States for jobs, more education, or both.

▲ **Some Muslim immigrants work as computer engineers.**

GROWING MUSLIM POPULATION IN THE UNITED STATES (2007-2017)

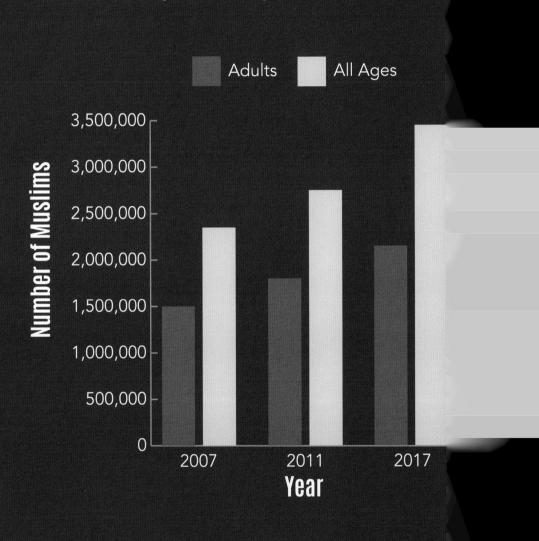

He was happy to have a good job. It helped his parents, too. He sent money to them in India every month. Still, sometimes it was hard to be in the United States. Even though he met many other Muslims, he found that different people worshipped in different ways. Some Muslims had taken on American ways and did not follow the Islamic calls for prayers or worship regularly. Others had no interest in getting to know Americans. They wanted to keep themselves separate. They believed that the United States was not a place where Islam could grow and flourish.

He was also shocked by some American behaviors. In the 1960s, some young Americans were rebelling. The young man saw people dressed in ways that would not have been allowed in his home. He felt the young Americans did not show the kind of respect to their elders that he had been raised to expect. He worried that his beliefs would not be accepted. However, the young man decided to stay in the United States despite the cultural differences he encountered.

◄ **Many Muslims are taught to help members of the older generations.**

Chapter 4

TWENTY-FIRST CENTURY MUSLIM IMMIGRANTS

The young girl was scared. She had never been on a plane before. Now she was strapped onto a gray cushioned plane seat. Her mother, two brothers, and sister were on the plane, too. They were going to the United States.

◄ **Approximately 31 percent of Muslims in the United States graduate from college. This is similar to the general population.**

Her aunt and uncle lived in Minneapolis, Minnesota. The girl did not know if Minneapolis was anything like Mogadishu, the capital of Somalia. She hoped that there would be enough food to eat there. She also hoped there would not be nights where she and her siblings huddled with their mother, scared of the sound of bombs outside their home.

At nine years old, all she could remember for much of her life was being hungry and afraid. She remembered the times her mother cried. Her mother was sad because there was no rain. When there was no rain, the garden did not grow. The goats died. They did not have enough to eat, and neither did their neighbors. Her brothers and sister cried. They were all weak from hunger and their stomachs hurt. Some of their neighbors died because there was no food.

Now they were going to the United States. Their aunt and uncle had sent money for them. She looked out the plane's window. The land below disappeared into soft white clouds.

When they got to their aunt and uncle's house, the young girl was amazed. Everything was green, from the trees to the grass in the yard. Inside the house, a large refrigerator was full of food. Her aunt greeted them and began cooking right away.

▲ Ilhan Omar came to the United States after fleeing
Somalia. She became the first Muslim Somali American
legislator after winning the 2016 election.

A big pot of water soon bubbled on the stove. Her aunt would
make pasta to go with the meat that browned in the skillet.
The young girl could smell onion, garlic, and pepper. It smelled
wonderful and she could hardly wait to eat.

The next day, they went for a walk. It was warm outside, with a nice breeze. Her aunt said that in the fall, they would go to school. In school they would have to speak English.

They stopped at the grocery store. The girl's aunt spoke to her in Somali as they paid for their food. A woman in line behind them suddenly yelled at them. She was angry that Muslim immigrants were coming to the United States. The little girl's aunt grabbed her arm and handed her a bag of groceries. Then the aunt pushed the little girl and her siblings out the door. She asked her aunt why the woman had yelled at them.

Her aunt looked sad. She told the girl that there were people in the United States who did not want Muslims in the country. She also said it had become worse since the terrorist attacks on September 11, 2001. That was when members of a terrorist group from Central Asia crashed planes into buildings in New York City and Washington, DC.

"When I was little . . . my dad and grandpa would talk to me about the possibility of coming to the United States, they would talk about the land of liberty and justice for all."[4]

— *Ilhan Omar, a Muslim woman from Somalia and a U.S. politician*

▲ **Many Somali parents seek better lives for their families in the United States.**

The attacks caused some people to believe all Muslims wanted to hurt Americans, even though that was not true.

The girl thought about what her aunt said. All the girl wanted was to feel safe and not be hungry. She did not want her mother to cry because there was no rain. She did not want her brothers and sisters to cry because they were starving.

Several years later, the girl waited patiently with her family at a courthouse. The family was there for a special ceremony.

They were about to take an oath of **allegiance** to the United States. That was the final step in becoming U.S. citizens. Through the many months of working to become citizens, the girl had seen some people who did not like Muslims. But she had also met people who were friendly. The girl had made friends in her school. Her family felt safe, and they had enough to eat. Their mother had found a job and was saving money to find a home of their own. The girl was excited to become a U.S. citizen. Even though there had been some hard times, her life was much better in the United States. Every day she prayed that all Americans would be safe from harm.

THINK ABOUT IT

- Why do you think it's important for people to be able to practice their religion in the United States?
- Why do you think some Muslim immigrants decide to leave after they have lived in the United States?
- What do you think is the most difficult part about moving to another country?

GLOSSARY

allegiance (uh-LEE-juhns): Allegiance means giving full loyalty to a person, group, cause, or country. Immigrants who become U.S. citizens have to pledge their allegiance to the United States.

alms (AHLMS): Alms are food or money given to needy people. Some Muslims gave alms to the poor.

Arabic (AIR-uh-bik): Arabic is a language spoken by many people in North Africa and the Middle East. Some Muslim immigrants taught themselves how to read Arabic.

homeland (HOME-land): Someone's homeland is their native land, or where they were born. Some Muslim immigrants didn't feel safe in their homeland, the Ottoman Empire.

mosques (MOSKS): Places of Muslim worship are known as mosques. Muslim people build mosques so they can have a large space to practice their religion.

Muslim (MUHZ-lim): A Muslim is a person who worships in the Islam faith. Many Muslim immigrants live in the United States.

peddlers (PED-lerz): Peddlers sell things door to door. Some Muslim immigrants worked as peddlers.

Quran (koor-AHN): The Quran is the sacred book of the Islam faith. Many Muslims study the messages in the Quran.

SOURCE NOTES

1. "The Mother Mosque and the Muslim Community in Cedar Rapids, Iowa: An American Story." *Pluralism Project*. Harvard University, 2016. Web. 14 Aug. 2018.

2. Ibid.

3. Kambiz GhaneaBassiri. *A History of Islam in America: From the New World to the New World Order*. New York, NY: Cambridge UP, 2010. 184.

4. Kenzi Abou-Sabe. "Ilhan Omar Likely to be First Somali-American Muslim Woman in Elected Office." *NBC News*. NBC Universal, 7 Nov. 2016. Web. 17 Aug. 2018.

TO LEARN MORE

Books

Barnard, Bryn. *The Genius of Islam: How Muslims Made the Modern World*. New York, NY: Alfred A. Knopf, 2011.

Hutchison, Patricia. *Somali Immigrants: In Their Shoes*. Mankato, MN: The Child's World, 2018.

Rose, Simon. *Sheikh Zayed Grand Mosque*. New York, NY: Weigl, 2014.

Web Sites

Visit our Web site for links about Muslim immigrants:

childsworld.com/links

Note to Parents, Teachers, and Librarians: We routinely verify our Web links to make sure they are safe and active sites. So encourage your readers to check them out!

INDEX